MW00770258

# *A TIME*

# *TO SEEK*

# *GOD*

*Truths compiled
from the writings of*

# FRANCIS
# FRANGIPANE

ISBN #1-886296-00-6

# CONTENTS

# PREFACE

We have come to realize the one great need of the church is to find God. In your personal pursuit, we trust these messages will help supply you with grace, inspiration, and direction. It is our prayer that you will seek and find the fullness of God.

# *1.*

# THE TENT OF MEETING

*"When Thou didst say, 'Seek My face,' my heart said to Thee, 'Thy face, O Lord, I shall seek' " (Ps 27:8).*

## A Time to Seek God

There are certain times when the Lord calls us out of the routine of our daily lives. These are special seasons where His only command is, **"Seek My face."** He has something precious and vitally important to give us that the familiar pattern of our daily devotions cannot accommodate. During such times, people are often delivered of sins that have plagued them for years; others discover a depth in their walk with God that leads to greater effectiveness in ministry and prayer; still others experience breakthroughs in their families and are used by God to see loved ones brought into the Kingdom.

Yet, the highest form of seeking God is not for personal needs or even for other people. We are seeking God for Himself. Maturity starts as we break the cycle of seeking God only during hardship; holiness begins the moment we seek God for Himself. A touch from God is wonderful, but we are in pursuit of more than just an experience—more than "goose bumps and tears." *We are seeking a place of abiding in Christ, where we are attentively aware of His glory within us.*

How do we enter this sacred place? If we study the life of Moses, we will see how he sought God and lived in fellowship with Him.

> **Now Moses used to take the tent and pitch it outside the camp, a good distance from the camp, and he called it the tent of meeting. And it came about, that everyone who sought the Lord would go out to the tent of meeting which was outside the camp (Ex 33:7).**

Notice that **"everyone who sought the Lord would go out."** If we are going to truly seek the Lord, we must **"go out"** as did Moses and those who sought the Lord. We must pitch our tent **"a good distance from the camp."** What camp is this? For Moses, as well as for us, it is the "camp of familiarity."

Is there anything inherently wrong or sinful about the things that are familiar? No, not in themselves, but you will remember that when Jesus told His disciples to follow Him, He called them to leave the familiar pattern of their lives for extended periods and be alone with Him (see Matthew 19:27). Why? Because He knew that men, by nature, are unconsciously governed by the familiar. If He is to expand us to receive the eternal, He must rescue us from the limitations of the temporal.

This is not to say we neglect our families, or that we become irresponsible as we seek God. No. God has given everyone enough time to seek Him. Having done what love would have us do for our families, we simply say no to every other voice but God's. We *redeem* the time: cancel hobbies, forsake television, put away the newspaper and magazines. Those who desire to find God, find time.

Sadly, many Christians have no higher goal, no greater aspiration, than to become "normal." Their desires are limited to measuring up to others. Without a true vision of God, we most certainly will perish spiritually! Paul rebuked the church at Corinth because they walked, **"like mere men"** (1 Cor 3:3). God has more for us than merely becoming better people; He wants to flood our lives with the same power that raised Christ from the dead! We must understand: God does not merely want us "normal"; He wants us Christlike!

For the Holy Spirit to facilitate God's purposes in our lives, He must redefine both our definition of reality and our priorities in life. Christlikeness must become our singular goal.

For most of us, however, our sense of reality and, thus, our security are rooted in the familiar. How difficult it is to grow spiritually if our security is based upon the stability of outward things! Our peace must come from God, not circumstances, nor even relationships. Our sense of reality needs to be rooted in Christ. When it is, the other areas of our life experience God's security.

Yet, our fears run deep and are many. Indeed, most of us pass through life umbilically tied to the protection of the familiar. Experience tells us that many good people remain in lifeless churches simply because they desire the security of familiar faces more than the truth of Christ. Why is it that people who have been delivered from adverse situations are often drawn back into similar situations? *Because adversity is more familiar to them.* Consider that certain prisoners are repeat offenders simply because they are more accustomed to prison life than freedom. Sadly, it is often true that young girls, having been abused by their fathers, tend to seek out and marry men who similarly abuse them. Groping blindly through life, they seek for the familiar.

It is significant that, worldwide, most people live within fifty miles of their birthplaces. Humans are cocooned, insulated against change, by the familiar. When we work all day only to come home, watch television, and then collapse in bed, our lifestyle becomes a chain of bondage. These things may not necessarily trap us in sin as much as they distract us from God.

Moses would leave what was familiar and pitch his tent **"outside the camp,"** where he would then seek the Lord.

> **Therefore Jesus also, that He might sanctify the people through His own blood, suffered outside the gate. Hence, let us go out to Him outside the camp, bearing His reproach. For here we do not have a lasting city, but we are seeking the city which is to come** (Heb 13:12-14).

In the same way that Moses and those who sought the Lord went outside the camp, and as Jesus went outside the camp, so also must we, at times, leave the camp of what seems normal and predictable, and set our hearts after God. Here we do not have a lasting city, but we are seeking the city which is to come.

This is one reason why Jesus said, **"when you pray, go into your inner room, and when you have shut your**

**door, pray"** (Matt 6:6). *Christ desires us to leave the distracting familiar world of our senses and abide in the world of our hearts, bearing in mind that the highest goal of prayer is to find God.*

Every minute you seek God is a minute enriched with new life, new power from God. Give yourself a minimum amount of time—an hour or two each day, but do not set a maximum, as the Lord may draw you to seek Him on into the night. And continue day by day, week by week, until you have drawn near enough to God that you can hear His voice, becoming confident that He is close enough to you to hear your whisper (see James 4:8).

If we are going to become holy, we must sever the chains and restraints—the bondage of desiring just an average life. We will choose to leave the camp of familiarity and place our tent in the Presence of God.

# 2.

# *Two Things, Two Things Only*

*There are so many things to occupy
our minds: so many books, so many
examples, so many good teachings that
deserve our attention, that say "Here is
a truth." But, as I have been serving the
Lord these past years, He has led me to
seek for two things, and two things only:
to know the heart of God in Christ, and
to know my own heart in Christ's light.*

## Knowing the Heart of God

I have been seeking God, searching
to know Him and the depth of love He
has for people. I want to know Christ's
heart and the compassions that motivate

Him. The Scriptures are plain: Jesus loved people. Mark's gospel tells us that after He taught and healed the multitudes, they became hungry. In His compassion, Christ saw them as **"sheep without a shepherd"** (Mark 6:34). It was not enough for Him to heal and teach them; He personally cared for each of them. Their physical well-being, even concerning food, was important to Him.

A lad with five loaves and two fish provided enough for Jesus to work a miracle, but this miracle had to come through Christ's bone-weary, but willing, body. Consider: Christ brought His disciples out to *rest*, **"For there were many people coming and going, and they did not even have time to eat"** (Mark 6:31). Consider: Jesus personally had come to pray and be strengthened; John the Baptist, Jesus' forerunner, had been beheaded earlier that very week at the hands of Herod. It was in the state of being emotionally and physically depleted that Jesus fed the multitudes—not just once or twice, but throughout the day over and over again, **"He kept giving them to the disciples to set before them"** (Mark 6:41).

*Thousands* of men, women, and children all **"ate and were satisfied"**! Oh, the heart of Jesus! The miracle was for them, but we read of no miracle sustaining Him except the marvelous wonder of a holy love that continually lifted His tired hands with more bread, more fish. Out of increasing weakness He repeatedly gave that others might be strengthened!

Jesus loves people—all people, especially those whom society ignores. Therefore, I must know exactly how far He would travel for men, for that is the same distance He would journey again through me! I must know His thoughts concerning illness, poverty, and human suffering! As His servant, I am useless to Him unless I know these things. If I am to actually do His will, I must truly know His heart. Thus, in all my study and times of prayer I am seeking for more than facts about God: I am searching for His heart.

## Knowing Our Hearts

At the same time, while I draw closer to the heart of God, the very fire of His Presence begins a deep purging work within me. In the vastness of His riches, my poverty appears. The psalmist wrote,

> **Who may ascend into the hill of the Lord? And who may stand in His holy place? He who has clean hands and a pure heart, who has not lifted up his soul to falsehood, and has not sworn deceitfully** (Ps 24:3-4).

We cannot even find the hill of the Lord, much less ascend it, if there is deceit in our soul. How does one serve in God's holy place if his heart is unclean? *It is only the pure in heart who perceive God.* To ascend toward God is to walk into a furnace of truth, where falsehood is extracted from our souls. To abide in the holy place we must dwell in honesty, even when a lie might seem to save us. Each ascending step upon the hill of God is a thrusting of our souls into greater transparency, a more perfect view into the motives of our hearts.

It is this upward call of God which we pursue (see Philippians 3:14). Yet, the soul within us is hidden, crouching in fears and darkness, living in a world of untruths and illusions. This is our inner man, the soul God seeks to save. Have you seen your inner person whom truth alone can free? Yes, we seek holiness, but true holiness arises from here, in the hidden place of our hearts. Indeed, it is *truthfulness* which leads to *holiness!* God, grant us a zeal for truth, that we may stand in Your holy place!

Men everywhere presume they know the "truth," but have neither holiness nor power in their lives. Truth must become more than historical doctrines; it must be more than a museum of religious arti-facts—mementos from when God once moved. Truth is knowing God's heart as it was revealed in Christ, and it is know-ing our own hearts in the light of God's grace.

As members of the human race, we are shrouded in ignorance. Barely do we know our world around us; even less do we know our own hearts. Without real-izing it, as we search for God's heart, we are also searching for our own. For it is only in finding Him that we discover ourselves; we are "in Him."

Yet, throughout that searching process, as I position my heart before Him, it is with a sense of trembling that I pray the prayer of King David,

**Search me, O God, and know my heart; try me and know my anxious thoughts; and see if there be any hurtful way in me, and lead me in the everlasting way** (Ps 139:23-24).

Let us wash the cosmetics from our souls and look at the reality of our hearts. I know God has created us eternally complete and perfect in Christ. I believe that. But in the first three chapters of John's Revelation, Jesus did not tell the churches they were "perfect in His eyes." No! He revealed to them their hearts; He told them their sins. Without compromise, He placed on them the demand to be overcomers, each in his own unique and difficult circumstance. Like those in the early church, we must know our need. And like them, the souls we want saved dwell here, in time, in a world system structured by lies, illusions, and rampant corruption. Our old natures are like well-worn shoes into which we relax; we can be in the flesh instantly without even realizing it. The enemies which defeat us are hidden and latent within us! *The Holy Spirit must expose our foes before we can conquer them!*

Concerning man's nature, we are told that, **"The heart is more deceitful than all else, and is desperately sick. Who can understand it?"** (Jer 17:9) Quoting David again, a similar cry is heard,

> **Who can discern his errors? Acquit me of hidden faults. Also keep back thy servant from presumptuous sins; let them not rule over me; then I shall be blameless, and I shall be acquitted of great transgression** (Ps 19:12-13).

There may be errors inside of us that are actually ruling us without our awareness. Do we realize, for instance, how many of our actions are manipulated purely by vanity and the desire to be accepted by others? Are we aware of the fears and apprehensions that unconsciously influence so many of our decisions? We may have serious problems inside, yet still be either too proud or too insecure to admit we need help. Concerning ourselves, we think so highly of that which we know so little!

Even outwardly, though we know our camera pose, do we know how we appear when we are laughing or crying, eating or sleeping, talking or angry? The fact is, most of us are ignorant of how we appear outwardly to others; much less do we know ourselves inwardly before God! Our fallen thinking processes automatically justify our actions and rationalize our thoughts. Without the Holy Spirit, we

*our fallen thinking processes*
*Justify our actions & rationalize our thoughts*

are nearly defenseless against our own innate tendencies toward self-deception!

Therefore, if we are to be holy, we must first renounce falsehood. *In the light of God's grace, having been justified by faith and washed in the sacrificial blood of Jesus, we need not pretend to be righteous. We need only to become truthful.*

No condemnation awaits our honesty of heart; no punishment. We have only to repent and confess our sins to have them forgiven and cleansed. We need merely to love and embrace the truth to be delivered from sin and self-deception. We need to know two things and two things only: the heart of God in Christ, and our own hearts in Christ's light.

# 3.

# UNRELENTING LOVE

*The Bible describes our relationship with the Lord Jesus in strong symbolic pictures of oneness: He is Head of a body, Husband of a wife, God in His temple. In spite of these and other powerful metaphors, there remains a sense of distance between the Presence of the Lord and ourselves. This distance is a test. Our call is to possess that love of God which reaches even into eternity and brings the glory and Person of Christ back to the church.*

## Seeking God

**"God has looked down from heaven upon the sons of men, to see if there is anyone who understands, who seeks after God"** (Ps 53:2). We simply must have more of Jesus. In the face of increasing wickedness in the world, our programs and ideas have failed. We need God. Those "who understand" are seeking Him. The wise know that Christ Himself is our only strategy and hope.

True understanding comes from seeking the Lord. Thus, we will explore the Song of Solomon, for here we find a bride and bridegroom who both are intolerant of the distance between them. The bride in the passage symbolizes the church in her deepest longings for Jesus; the Bridegroom in the story is Christ. We will start with the third chapter; the bride is speaking.

**"On my bed night after night I sought him whom my soul loves"** (Song 3:1). True seeking of God is born out of love. Our quest for God is not a matter of discipline, but of desire; it is not a question of sacrifice, but of undistracted love. Your sleep is gone because your beloved is gone. You *must* seek Him, for such is the nature of love.

Some will say, "But I already know the Lord. I have found Him." In truth, it was He who found us. Our salvation rests securely upon this fact. But while many in the church are resting upon what Christ has done, the bride seeks to be with Jesus, to "find" deep and intimate fellowship with Him. In the very love which Christ inspired, she arises to find Him.

There is yet much more to learn and discover concerning our Lord. At the end of Moses' life, after being used by God to confront and defeat the gods of Egypt, after dwelling in His glory for 40 years, Moses prays, **"Thou hast *begun* to show Thy servant Thy greatness and Thy strong hand"** (Deut 3:24). For all we may think we know, we have barely found but a thimbleful of His glory. **"As many as are perfect, have this attitude"** (Phil 3:15). Seeking God is the attitude of the mature; it is the attitude of Christ's bride.

In this maturation process, there will come a point when, within the heart of the bride, love for God takes ascendancy over mere intellectual or doctrinal understanding. She cannot contain her longing nor patronize her aching heart by saying, "I will feel better in the morning." There simply is no reconciling the passion of her soul with the absence of her beloved.

Note also, there is an unfolding dimension to seeking the Lord which we must embrace. *Genuine love for God is an unrelenting hunger.* As you would die without food, so you feel you will die without Him. She says, **"night after night"** I sought him. The knowledge of what her beloved has done in the past, a "religion" about Him, will provide little solace for the bride. She wants Him!

## Overcoming Resistance

"**I sought him whom my soul loves. I sought him but did not find him**" (Song 3:1). There are many obstacles which hinder our truly finding the Lord. Augustine said it well, "God is not on the surface." There is a "**secret place of the most High**" (Ps 91:1 Ampl). Although hidden, it *is* an accessible place. But we must not stop short of His fullness, nor settle for only edification, encouragement, or comfort—the wonderful "effects" of Christ. We are seeking for more than "chills" and tears. We are searching for Jesus Himself.

Let us also understand that our pursuit of God is not an act, but an attitude. We will not find Him by searching only in convenient times and comfortable places. Rather, our quest is a restless, continual pilgrimage until we find Him. Our confidence is in His promise: the day we seek for Him with our whole hearts, we will find Him.

There is a story of a young man in search of God who came to study at the feet of an old teacher. The sage brought this young man to a lake, leading him out into the shoulder-deep water. Putting his hands upon his pupil's head, he promptly pushed him under the water and continued to hold him there until the disciple, feeling he would surely drown, desperately fought the old man's resistance. In shock and confusion, the young man resurfaced. His teacher looked him in the eyes and said, *"When you want God as much as you wanted air, you shall find Him."*

The question here is not only of desire, but of survival. How can I live without Him? Have we, in our society, comfortably adapted to a life apart from Him and then invented doctrinal opinions to justify our unbelief and indifference? In spite of our doctrines, Christ's promise is firm, **"If anyone loves Me, he will keep My word; and My Father will love him, and We will come to him, and make Our abode with him"** (John 14:23).

The bride continues, **"I must arise now and go about the city; in the streets and in the squares I must seek him whom my soul loves"** (Song 3:2). This inexorable woman has risen from the security of her own bed. She has left the comfort of her own house and is now seeking Christ in the streets and squares. Pastors, hear me: not all who wander from church to church are uncommitted or superficial Christians; a significant number are searching for their beloved. They are asking, *"Have you seen Him?"*

Yet, not only is the bride in the streets and squares of Christianity, but she is facing the force and the power of darkness as well. Nothing stops her—not her own need of sleep nor her own fear of the night. Her love exceeds her fear.

However, again she is refused. **"I sought him but did not find him"** (v 2).

We might think that after so great an expense of her energies, and even the seeming reluctance of heaven to answer her cry, she would feel dutifully justified to return home, but she does not. We too must guard against becoming satisfied with our opinion of ourselves: "We prayed, we waited, we searched for God. We did more than other men." This false reward fills the soul with self-exaltation. If we are to truly find Him, we must stay empty and hungry for God alone.

**"The watchmen who make the rounds in the city found me, and I said, 'Have you seen him whom my soul loves?'"** (v 3) From her bed, to the streets, and now to the watchmen, she is seeking her lover. Notice that the watchmen found *her.* The watchmen are the true prophetic ministries, the "seers." Their highest calling is to find the searching bride and direct her to Jesus. While many may come to the seers for a word of encouragement or revelation, the bride is looking for Jesus. Her singleness of purpose is undistracted; she asks the watchmen, *"Have you seen Him?"*

**"Scarcely had I left them when I found him whom my soul loves."** This is the greatest motivation for seeking the Lord: the time will come when you find Him! You will pass your tests and overcome the obstacles; you will be secure in the embrace of Christ. She says, **"I held on to him and would not let him go"** (Song 3:4). I am reminded of Mary

Magdalene at the empty tomb of Christ.
The apostles came, looked in the cave and
went away astounded. But Mary came to
the tomb and she lingered, weeping. The
death of Christ was horrible, but His
missing body was unspeakable. She could
not bear an empty tomb. She had to have
Him whom her soul loved!

The Scripture says that Jesus Himself
came behind her, but in her sorrow she
did not recognize Him. He said, **"Woman, why are you weeping? Whom are
you seeking?"** (John 20:15) Can we see
the connection here between Mary's
weeping and her seeking Christ? Suppos-
ing Him to be the gardener, she said, **"Sir,
if you have carried Him away, tell me
where you have laid Him, and I will
take Him away"** (v 15). She would settle
for a dead Jesus if she could just put her
arms around him!

> **Jesus said to her, "Mary!" She
> turned and said to Him in He-
> brew, "Rabboni!" (which means,
> Teacher). Jesus said to her,
> "Stop clinging to Me; for I have
> not yet ascended to the Father"**
> (John 20:16-17).

The instant Mary sees the Lord she
clings to Him. Jesus said, **"I have not yet
ascended."** And here is the most astound-
ing event, indeed, the marvel of all mar-
vels: *Jesus interrupted His ascent into
Heaven to answer this woman's love!* He
had not yet ascended, but in the process of
His resurrection, He is drawn—No!

*compelled*—toward her weeping! Jesus demonstrated that love is the highest, most compelling power of His kingdom!

When you expend your energies, your nights, your heart; when you overcome your fears out of love for Jesus, you will find Him and *"not let him go."* She has found him whom her soul loves. She continued in her pursuit, remaining in sorrow, until she found him. The church leaders went home. To whom did Jesus appear? He came to the one who had the highest passion for Him. And she is clinging to Him.

## Bringing Jesus to Our Mother's House

**"I found him whom my soul loves; I held on to him and would not let him go, until I had brought him to my mother's house, and into the room of her who conceived me"** (Song 3:4).

You have laid hold of Jesus; you have found fulfillment. Yet, has this seeking of God been only for you? No. For the bride brings Him back to the house of her mother, which is the church. She brings Him back to the needy and hurting, to her brothers and her sisters.

We all want the Lord, but only the bride will go so far as to find Him and bring Him back to the house. I want to charge you to find Jesus. Do not merely talk about how dead your life or church is, find Him! Pass through your fears.

Overcome your passivity and lay hold of Him. The church, our mother, needs Jesus!

Where was Jesus throughout the time of her searching? Was He aloof, indifferent, sitting in Heaven? No. From the beginning, He has been watching, actually longing for His bride to find Him. He now speaks. **"You have made my heart beat faster, my sister, my bride; you have made my heart beat faster with a single glance of your eyes"** (Song 4:9).

Listen: *You are His bride. He is returning from heaven for you!* The "single glance" of your eyes has made His heart beat faster. Such love is inconceivable. He sees your repentance as His bride making herself ready. He beholds you kneeling, weeping for Him at your bedside. He shares your painful longing. He has been watching. And he says, *"The glance of your eyes has made my heart beat faster."*

The Lord has a promise for His bride. He said there will be a fresh and overwhelming baptism of love that will surpass all our knowledge of Him. We will know the height and depth, the width and the breadth of His love. While yet here on earth, we will be filled with His fullness.

We have many tasks, even responsibilities, which have come from heaven. However, the need of our soul is to be with Jesus. The areas of sin in our life are there simply because we have lived too far from Him. Let us commit our hearts to seeking the Lord. Let us find Him whom our soul loves and bring Him back to our mother's house!

> [That you may really come] to know—practically, through experience for yourselves—the love of Christ, which far surpasses mere knowledge (without experience); that you may be filled (through all your being) unto all the fullness of God—[that is] may have the richest measure of the divine Presence, and become a body wholly filled and flooded with God Himself! (Eph 3:19 Ampl)

# 4.

# DRAWING NEAR TO THE HOLY GOD

*The Lord did not cease being holy when the New Testament began; His nature did not change. When Jesus taught His disciples to pray, He began with "hallowed be Thy Name." If we are to truly know Him as He is, we need an Old Testament fear of the Lord combined with the New Testament experience of His grace.*

## Understanding God's Holiness

Now when Solomon had finished praying, fire came down from heaven and consumed the burnt offering and the sacrifices; and the glory of the Lord filled the house. And the priests could not enter into the house of the Lord, because the glory of the Lord filled the Lord's house. And all the sons of Israel, seeing the fire come down and the glory of the Lord upon the house, bowed down on the pavement with their faces to the ground, and they worshipped and gave praise to the Lord** (2 Chron 7:1-3).

What an unparalleled event in the history of man! After Solomon dedicated the temple, the glory of the Lord descended and filled His house. What was this glory? It was the light, the bursting forth into man's world, of the radiant holiness of God Eternal. It signified that the Lord's actual Person had drawn near. So great was this appearance of glory that the priests could not enter the temple. After the fire fell and the Lord's glory filled the temple, we read, **"Then the king and all the people offered sacrifice before the Lord. And King Solomon offered a sacrifice of 22,000 oxen, and 120,000 sheep"** (2 Chron 7:4-5).

Consider this, that the king offered *22,000 oxen, 120,000 sheep!* They were not serving an invisible God by faith— they were in the manifested Presence of the Creator Himself! Solomon could have offered one million oxen, yet it would not have satisfied the demands of his eyes as he beheld the glory of God! *It is only our fathomless ignorance of Who the Lord truly is that suggests a limit on any sacrifice we bring Him.*

As Solomon's offering demonstrates, the more we see God as He is, the more compelled we are to give Him our all. Yet, herein lies a major problem that every present-day Christian must face: though most know of God intellectually, few know Him in His glory. Our churches tend to be sanctuaries of formality, not of the Divine Presence. If we are part of that sector of Christianity that departed from ritualism, what we offer in its place are merely varying degrees of informality. But where is God? Where is His creative, unlimited power in our gatherings? When was the last time our pastors could not stand to minister because the glory of God overwhelmed them? Such was the God of the Old Testament, the Holy One Christ revealed.

The Hebrew people knew God was holy—that was both their virtue and their problem, because He was *too* holy for them to face as sinful individuals. They served Him without relating to Him. For a vast majority of the Jews, their offerings were not born out of an eagerness to seek God's Presence as much as they were an effort to satisfy His unalterable justice (see Hebrews 2:1-2).

The common man never approached God Himself, but brought his required offerings to the local priests. The priests, in turn, had a multitude of regulations and preparations they needed to fulfill before they themselves could approach God. There were daily, weekly, and annual sacrifices; sin offerings and sacrifices of praise for harvests; as well as assigned offerings for restored health. Whatever the need, when the priests approached the Almighty, they could not come near without the shedding of blood or the offering of grain. They had washings, burning of incense, and the recitation of certain prayers, all which had to be fulfilled in precise detail with the most exacting adherence to the requirements of the Ceremonial Law.

To further illustrate the Old Testament perception of God, we are told in Leviticus that Aaron's priestly sons brought a "strange offering" to the Lord. When they did so, **"fire came out from the presence of the Lord and consumed them, and they died before the Lord"** (Lev 10:2). In consoling Aaron, Moses said, **"It is what the Lord spoke, saying, 'By those who come near Me I will be treated as holy' "**(Lev 10:3). And the Scripture says, **"So Aaron, therefore, kept silent"** (Lev 10:3). In Aaron's mind, the holiness of God justified the instant death of Aaron's unholy sons!

Ultimately, the relationship between God and the Hebrews was not one of fellowship; it was almost strictly a matter of proper ritual and obedience to the Law. Other than the prophets and a handful of

*Notes*

kings, few lived in harmony with the higher ways of God.

For us as Christians, through the blood of Jesus, God has opened the way to the holy place of His Presence (see Hebrews 10:19-22). For the Hebrews, however, only the high priest entered the holy place, and then, just once a year on the Day of Atonement. So fearful were the Levites of the consequences of violating God's unbending Law that, before the high priest entered the holy place, a rope was tied around his leg and small bells were sewn into his clothing. Thus, in the event he suddenly died or collapsed while in the holy of holies, the quieted bells alerted his fellow priests, enabling them to pull him from the sacred room without violating the Law.

What we perceive in the carefulness of the high priest characterizes the attitude of the Old Testament Jew: no one dared approach the holy, living Presence of God without perfectly fulfilling the Law. Eventually, the Jews stopped writing and speaking the sacred name of God. Even His name was too holy to be uttered in this world.

### Understanding God's Grace

This very sense of God's holiness is one of the main reasons why the first-century church in Jerusalem was so powerful. As Jews, they knew the holiness of God's law. But, as Christians they possessed the knowledge of His grace;

they personally knew the Lamb, the Perfect Sacrifice, who had come and fulfilled the requirements of the law. God, even He whom the Jews worshipped, had taken human form and given *Himself* for sin!

Many Christians the world over celebrate the forgiveness of sins in Christ, but they end their experience with God there. Jews, who knew historically the fearful justice of God, still lived outside the Divine Presence because they did not understand the forgiveness of sins in Christ. *But, it is the union of both truths that produces power in our lives and leads us into the reality of God.*

Abraham was about to sacrifice his beloved son, Isaac, to God. (Remember, anyone who has seen God as He is, willingly offers his all.) As they walked up the mountain, Abraham spoke prophetically. He said, **"God will provide for Himself the lamb"** (Gen 22:8). While we must be willing to give to God our all, we must remember that our all is not good enough. God has provided His own Son, the perfect Lamb, as access to Himself.

There are many times when we feel unworthy, when we seek to escape from the Person of God. In these times, the last one we want to face is God in His holiness. But in the midst of our unworthiness, let us call upon the Lord. We can escape *to* God for forgiveness.

When John the Baptist looked at Jesus, he told his disciples, **"Behold, the Lamb of God who takes away the sin**

*Notes*

of the world!" (John 1:29). The Lamb of God has taken away not just the sins of the world, but *your* sins as well. Christ's sacrifice is much more than all the bulls and sheep ever offered throughout all of time; He perfectly satisfies the demand of God's holy justice. And while the high priest drew near with fear and terror, we can draw near with confidence through the blood of Christ—so great and complete is the sacrifice God has provided! (see Hebrews 4:16)

The judgment of God's law is holy, but the sacrifice of the Son of God is more holy still, for **"mercy triumphs over judgment"** (James 2:13). The Lord who filled Solomon's temple with His Presence will fill, *and is filling,* His people today! We have the Inexhaustible Sacrifice Himself seated upon the Throne of Grace—it is He who is calling us to come boldly before Him! Enter, therefore, into His glory by the blood of the Lamb! Let Jesus wash your heart of its sins! For our goal is to live in the Presence of the very same Holy God who appeared in His glory to the Hebrews!

# 5.

# A PLACE FOR HIM TO REST

*In the Kingdom, there are no great men of God, just humble men whom God has chosen to use greatly. How do we know when we are humble? When God speaks, we tremble. God is looking for a man who trembles at His word. Such a man will find the Spirit of God resting upon him; he will become a dwelling place for the Almighty.*

### Entering the Sabbath Rest of God

**"Heaven is My throne, and the earth is My footstool. Where then is a house you could build for Me? And where is a place that I may rest?"**

(Isa 66:1) God asks for nothing but ourselves. Our beautiful church buildings, our slick professionalism, are nearly useless to God. He does not want what we have; He wants who we are. He seeks to create in our hearts a sanctuary for Himself, a place where He may rest.

In the Scriptures this "rest" is called "the Sabbath rest." It does not, however, come from keeping the Sabbath, for the Jews kept the Sabbath but they never entered God's rest. The book of Hebrews is plain: Joshua did not give the Israelites rest (see Hebrews 4:7-8). And after so long a period of time of Sabbath-keeping, the Scripture continues, **"There remains therefore a Sabbath rest for the people of God"** (Heb 4:9). This rest, therefore, was something beyond keeping the seventh day holy.

The question must be asked then, "What is this Sabbath rest?" Let us explore Genesis in pursuit of our answer. **"Then God blessed the seventh day and sanctified it, because in it He rested from all His work"** (Gen 2:3). Before God rested on the Sabbath, there was nothing special or holy about the seventh day. Had the Lord rested on the third day, then it would have been holy. *Rest is not in the Sabbath, it is in God.* Rest is a prevailing quality of His completeness.

Revelation 4:6 describes the throne of God as having before it, as it were, **"a sea of glass like crystal."** A sea of glass is a sea without waves or ripples, a symbol of the imperturbable calm of God. Let us grasp this point: *the Sabbath was not a source of rest for God; He was the Source of rest for the Sabbath.* As it is written, **"the Creator of the ends of the earth does not become weary or tired"** (Isa 40:28). And even as the Sabbath became holy when God rested upon it, so we become holy as we put away sin, as the fullness of God settles and rests upon us.

In our study, we are not associating God's rest merely with the sense of being rebuilt or rejuvenated, which we obviously need and associate with human rest. The rest we seek is not a rejuvenation of our energy, it is the *exchange* of energy; our life for God's, through which the vessel of our humanity is filled with the Divine Presence and all-sufficiency of Christ Himself.

### Enveloped and Permeated with God

The Hebrew word for "rest" was "nuach," and, among other things, it meant "to rest, remain, be quiet." It also indicated a "complete envelopment and thus permeation," as in the spirit of Elijah "resting" on Elisha, or when wisdom "rests in the heart of him who has understanding." God is not looking for a place where He can merely cease from His labors with men. He seeks a relationship where He can "completely envelop and thus permeate" every dimension of our lives, where He can tabernacle, remain, and be quiet upon us.

When our hearts have truly entered God's rest, we live in union with Jesus the same way He lived in union with the Father (see John 10:14-15). Christ's thought-life was "completely enveloped and thus permeated" with the Presence of God. He did only those things He saw and heard His Father do. He declared, **"the Father abiding in Me does His works"** (John 14:10). There is *rest* because it is *Christ working through us!* Jesus promises us, **"If you ask Me anything in My name, I will do it"** (John 14:14). How vain we are to think we can do miracles, love our enemies, or do any of the works of God without Christ doing His works through us!

This is why Jesus said, **"Come to Me . . . and I will give you rest"** (Matt 11:28). In a storm-tossed boat on the sea of Galilee, Christ's terrified disciples came to Him. Their cries were the cries of men about to die. Jesus rebuked the tempest, and immediately the wind and sea **"became perfectly calm"**; even as calm as He was (Matt 8:26). What program, what degree of ministerial professionalism, can compare with the life and power we receive through Him?

You see, our efforts, no matter how much we spend of ourselves, cannot produce the rest or life of God. *We must come to Him.* Many leaders have worked themselves nearly to exhaustion as they seek to serve God. If they spent half their time *with Him,* in prayer and waiting before Him, they would find His supernatural accompaniment working mightily in their efforts. They would become passengers in the vehicle of His will, a vehicle in which He Himself is both Captain and Navigator.

## Cease Striving, Know, Then Obey

To enter God's rest requires we abide in full surrender to His will, in perfect trust of His power. We learn to rest from our works **"as God did from His"** (Heb 4:10). It requires diligence, however, to enter God's rest (Heb 4:11). To "rest from our labors" does not mean we have stopped working; it means we have stopped the laborious work of the flesh and sin. It means we have entered the eternal works which He brings forth through us.

The turmoil caused by unbelief is brought to rest by faith. The strife rooted in unforgiveness is removed by love. Our fearful thoughts are arrested through trust in Him; our many questions are answered by His wisdom. Such is the mind which has entered the rest of God.

The church needs to possess the knowledge of God's ways, for herein do we enter His rest (see Hebrews 3:8-11). We gain such knowledge through obedience to God's Word during conflicts. As we obey God through the testings of life, we learn how to deal with situations as

God would. Consequently, it is of the utmost value to hear what God is speaking to us, and especially so when life seems to be a wilderness of hardship and trials.

Therefore, the Spirit says,

**"Today if you hear His voice, do not harden your hearts as when they provoked Me, as in the day of trial in the wilderness . . . Therefore I was angry with this generation, and said, 'They always go astray in their heart; and they did not know My ways'; as I swore in My wrath, they shall not enter My rest"** (Heb 3:7-11).

He says, **"they always go astray in their heart . . . they did not know My ways . . . they shall not enter My rest."** *Knowing God's ways leads to His rest.* We must see that there is no rest in a hardened heart. There is no rest when we rebel against God. Our rest comes from becoming honest about our needs and allowing Christ to change us.

Thus Jesus said, **"Learn from Me . . . and you shall find rest for your souls"** (Matt 11:29). Stop fighting with God and learn from Him! Let His Word put to death the torments of the sin nature. Cease struggling, cease wrestling against the Blessed One. Trust Him! For eventually His word will plunder the defenses of your heart. Be committed to the process of surrender! In time He shall no longer use adversity to reach your heart, for you shall delight in being vulnerable to Him. Continue your diligent yielding until even His whisper brings sweet trembling to your soul. Far more precious than the men of a hundred nations is one man perfectly given to the Spirit of God. This man is God's tabernacle, the one to whom God looks and is well pleased.

He says,

**"Heaven is My throne, and the earth is My footstool. Where then is a house you could build for Me? And where is a place that I may rest? For My hand made all these things, thus all these things came into being"** (Isa 66:1-2).

Yet, incredibly, one man with one quality of heart captures the attention and promise of God. **"But to this one I will look, to him who is humble and contrite of spirit, and who trembles at My word"** (Isa 66:2).

God looks to the man who trembles when He speaks. For in him the holy power of the Most High can abide in perfect peace. He has learned the ways of God; he delights in obedience. He has chosen to give God what He asks: nothing less than all he is. In return, this man becomes a place, a holy place, where God Himself can rest.

# 6.

# THE WAY INTO THE HOLY PLACE

*In the chronicles of the restoration of the church, it will be noted that a time came when the saints ceased being satisfied with their song services, when the deepest longings of their hearts ascended beyond the sounds of shouts and hand-clapping, a transitional time when pure worship began to carry them into the actual Presence of God.*

## We Are the Temple of God

This message is a brief study of the book of Hebrews. Except for certain chapters, the central message of Hebrews has been a mystery to most twentieth-century Christians. This is because it was originally written "to the Hebrews," people who were familiar with the tabernacle of God and the significance of the Divine Presence in the inner court of the tabernacle. We will be exploring the similarities between the outer and inner courts of the Hebrew tabernacle and the "outer and inner courts" of the New Testament tabernacle: *the Spirit-filled man.* Both have a sacred place which was created for the Presence of God. And both have a prescribed way to enter the Sacred Presence.

Paul tells us, **"Examine yourselves! Or do you not recognize this about yourselves, that Jesus Christ is in you?"** (2 Cor 13:5) Again, we are challenged, **"Do you not know that you are a temple of God, and that the Spirit of God dwells in you?"** (1 Cor 3:16) And again, Jesus, speaking for both Himself and God the Father, promised, **"If anyone loves Me, he will keep My word; and My Father will love him, and We will come to him, and make Our abode with him"** (John 14:23).

Such statements are so bold that most Bible teachers refuse to deal with them for fear of being accused of heresy. Yet, the incredible reality of God's Word cannot be altered in spite of compromise within the church. The holy meaning of the Word stands towering above men's traditions and unbelief. There is an **"upward call of God in Christ Jesus"**

(Phil 3:14). We must not ignore or rush past any of God's words. Rather, we encourage you to take time with this study, to dwell in it. For if you receive it properly, a door will swing open before you into the secret place of the Most High.

## The Outer and Inner Rooms

In your spirit is the Spirit of God. You are eternally saved not because you accepted the religion, Christianity, but because you have accepted the actual Spirit of Jesus Christ into your heart. Through Him you are able to come to God.

There is a place in your spirit where Christ actually dwells, an abiding place where His Holy Spirit and your human spirit literally touch. This is not merely a doctrine of faith, it is a matter of fact. This place is a holy place. We accept this truth because it is biblical. But how do we gain access to this holy place? And, once entered, is it possible to dwell there continually? The book of Hebrews provides us with an answer. In chapter nine we read, **"The Holy Spirit is signifying this, that the way into the holy place has not yet been disclosed, while the outer tabernacle is still standing"** (Heb 9:8).

There is a way to enter God's Presence, but this way is not revealed as long as the outer tabernacle is still standing. What is this "outer tabernacle"? For the

Jews, the outer tabernacle was the larger of the two rooms in the sacred tent. In this room we find the lampstand, the table, and the sacred bread (see Hebrews 9:2). It was also the first room the priests entered as they ministered the daily worship service (see Hebrews 9:6). A second inner room was also in the tent. This room was entered through a veil once a year by the high priest, not without taking blood, which he offered for himself and the sins of the people (see Hebrews 9:7). This was the Holy of Holies, the dwelling place of God on earth. In this room dwelt His Manifest Presence. God did not dwell in the "outer tabernacle"; He dwelt in the inner room.

The outer and inner rooms of the Jewish tabernacle symbolize our own outer and inner natures. Our "outer tabernacle" is our soul-life, constituting the view of life as seen through the mind and emotions (the soul) of man. In the outer tabernacle of our soul, our focus is outward. Worship consists of something we "perform" through a proper adherence to the ritual of our particular form of worship, according to our denomination or sect. It is that part of us that keeps us in church because of duty rather than vision. It leads us by our traditions instead of being led by the Spirit.

Rarely, if ever, does one experience the actual Presence of the Living God in the outer tabernacle. We may be saved by *faith,* but by *experience* the Presence of God seems far removed. What is experienced is a myriad of different ideas, emotionalism (or lack thereof), and much confusion concerning church order, eschatology and systems of worship. As long as man is ruled by circumstances rather than God, his "outer tabernacle" is still standing. No matter how zealous he seems, until the strength of his outer man is broken and an inner desire to worship and know God arises, the *way* into the holy place remains hidden.

Continuing the parallels between the Jewish tabernacle and human nature, the Bible tells us there was also an "inner tabernacle" which the Scriptures call the Holy of Holies. This inner tabernacle corresponds to the spiritual side of man. As it was in the physical temple, so it is in the temple of flesh: the Presence of God dwells in the inner tabernacle. In the physical temple, the inner tabernacle was so sacred, so holy, that great care was expended before it could be entered. No one casually entered the holy place. Into this inner tabernacle **"the high priest enters, once a year, not without taking blood, which he offers for himself and for the sins of the people committed in ignorance"** (Heb 9:7).

This inner tabernacle was the most sacred place on earth, for the manifested Presence of Yahweh, God of Israel, dwelt in this sacred room. When we think of entering the reality of God's Presence, we are immediately confronted with the depth of our sinfulness. How shall we approach God and live?

Yet, for us, the way into the holy place is not through self improvement, keeping the law, or any similar delusion. We enter the Presence of God through our relationship with Jesus Christ. God is not seeking to perfect us, but rather to perfect our *relationship* with Jesus. He is our Way into the Holy Place. He said, **"no one comes to the Father, but through Me"** (John 14:6). Christ's expressed purpose is to bring us **"to the Father."** Most Christians place this promise in the hereafter. But Jesus came to reconcile us to God in the *here and now*. Do not let this truth escape you! Many of the images, ideas, and traditions we have used to define Christianity have a certain degree of deception in them, not because they are not true, but because they do not go far enough into the will and provision of God!

The Scriptures tell us that, **"Through Him we . . . have our access in one Spirit to the Father"** (Eph 2:18). The Word proclaims that we are **"a holy temple in the Lord; in whom** [we] **also are being built together into a dwelling of God in the Spirit"** (Eph 2:21-22). We are God's holy temple, His habitation in the Spirit, and it is **"access . . . to the Father,"** where the Eternal One actually communes with us, that we are seeking.

But for what purpose do we seek God? We seek God to worship Him. Jesus said the Father is seeking worshippers. *The worship that satisfies God must originate from the Holy of Holies, where the consciousness of man is awakened to the Spirit of God.* Worship does not come from any system or form of service. Rather, it is the result of having truly discovered the Almighty One in **"spirit and truth"** (John 4:23).

## The New and Living Way

Because of sin and shame, every man places some sort of barrier between God and himself. The Bible refers to three instances of a veil separating the Jews from God. The first was the veil in the Hebrew temple. Here, only once a year, and only one man, the anointed high priest, could enter through the thick curtain (called the "veil") into God's holy place. This is the veil that was rent in two when Jesus died (see Matthew 27:51). This veil not only separated the outer room from the inner room of the tabernacle, *it had separated the world of men from the Presence of God.*

A second veil is mentioned, which Moses put over his face after having been with God. Once again we see the veil being used to separate the people from the glory of God, even though the glory on Moses' face would soon fade (see Exodus 34:29-35).

However, Paul tells us of a third veil, less perceptible than the others and, therefore, more dangerous. This is the veil which remains unlifted, not only from the hearts of the Jews, but from all who know not God (2 Cor 4:3-4). This is the veil of which the apostle says, **"but whenever a man turns to the Lord, the veil is taken away"** (2 Cor 3:16).

This third veil is the veil of our self-life. When the veil of self cloaks our hearts, our perceptions are stained by the basic selfish orientation of our nature. But when one turns to the Lord, the veil of self-life, like the veil in the temple, is rent in two. This is not the cutting of some thin fabric, but the rending of the heart, the splitting in two of the tightly woven fabric of self-righteousness and self-conscious-ness. It is a violent rending, a putting to death of the old self-nature.

Only if the old self-life is crucified without mercy or regret can the soul reach the state of purity where it perceives the Living God. In Moses we see a man *unveiled* before the Presence of God. When he returned to the sacred tent, he would remove the veil from his face, turn, and step through the curtain of veils into the brilliant glory of God. Here, the Scrip-tures tell us, in the radiance of Eternal Life, Moses spoke to God face to face.

In like manner, *the very same Sacred Presence now dwells in the inner taber-nacle of our spirits.* In Christ, with our veils of self, sin, and shame rent open, we too can turn and face God's glory—only the glory we face is not outside us. Nor does it fade from our faces as we depart

*Notes*

from it. The Spirit of God dwells within us. And every time we truly behold Him, each time He is revealed to us, our hearts change in ever-increasing degrees of glory, transforming us from glory unto glory into His same divine image (see Second Corinthians 3:18).

## The Veil of Christ's Flesh

In the light of such staggering spiritual realities, it is no wonder Satan fights the fulfillment of God's Word. Yet, God has provided not just the hope of receiving His nature, but also the means to attain it. The Father has provided a perfect offering, a sacrifice that for all time satisfies the penalty of sin, an offering that enables us to enter **"through the veil, that is His** [Christ's] **flesh"** into the glorious Presence of God (Heb 10:20).

You see, the final veil through which we pass is not made of linen; it is the fleshly body of Jesus Christ. We return to God through Him. The Scriptures tell us, **"If we confess our sins, He is faithful and righteous to forgive us our sins and to cleanse us from all unrighteousness"** (1 John 1:9).

The Word continues,

**I am writing these things to you that you may not sin. And if anyone sins, we have an Advocate with the Father, Jesus Christ the righteous; and He Himself is the propitiation for our sins** (1 John 2:1-2).

It is through Jesus' blood sacrifice that we are perfectly forgiven and thoroughly cleansed as we enter the Presence of God. When Christ was resurrected, He entered into the greater and more perfect tabernacle, not made with hands, that is to say, not of this creation (see Hebrews 9:11). When Jesus entered this true heavenly tabernacle, of which Moses' tabernacle was a copy, He did not take the blood of goats and calves; *He took His own shed blood into the holy place* (Heb 9:12-14).

Again, the book of Hebrews gives the best picture.

> **Therefore even the first covenant was not inaugurated without blood. For when every commandment had been spoken by Moses to all the people . . . he took the blood of the calves and the goats, with water and scarlet wool and hyssop, and sprinkled both the book itself and all the people, saying, "This is the blood of the covenant which God commanded you." And in the same way he sprinkled both the tabernacle and all the vessels of the ministry with the blood. And according to the Law . . . all things are cleansed with blood, and without shedding of blood there is no forgiveness** (Heb 9:18-22).

Under the Old Covenant, Moses sprinkled the blood of sacrificed animals upon everything in the holy place. *Through the sprinkled blood he cleansed the basic uncleanness that exists in all created things.* What Moses did through the sprinkling of blood in the earthly tabernacle, Jesus has done for us with His own blood in the heavenly tabernacle.

**Therefore it was necessary for the copies of the things in the heavens to be cleansed with these [blood], but the heavenly things themselves with better sacrifices than these. For Christ did not enter a holy place made with hands, a mere copy of the true one, but into heaven itself** (Heb 9:23-24).

Apart from you and I, there is nothing else in the heavenly tabernacle that is defiled. *We are the "heavenly things" that needed cleansing with Christ's blood before we could enter the true tabernacle.* As Moses cleansed the earthly copy of the holy place with blood, so Jesus cleanses the people who enter the true tabernacle with Him in heaven.

During the Passover meal Jesus took the symbolic cup of wine and told His disciples, **"Drink from it, all of you; for this is My blood of the covenant, which is poured out for many for forgiveness of sins"** (Matt 26:27-28). Hebrews tells us this sacrifice was so perfect that **"by one offering He has** perfected for all time those who are [being] sanctified" (Heb 10:14). When Jesus agreed to die for man, essentially what He said to the Father was, "Every time they sin, and for every kind of sin they commit, as long as there is repentance and faith in their hearts, My life is given for their redemption."

> Since therefore, brethren, we have confidence to enter the holy place by the blood of Jesus, by a new and living way which He inaugurated for us through the veil, that is, His flesh, and since we have a great priest over the house of God, let us draw near with a sincere heart in full assurance of faith (Heb 10:19-22).

The call and desire of God is for our worship to be in Spirit and in Truth. *Through the provision of Jesus Christ, we can be as close to God as our desires will take us. The limits are not on God's side, but on ours.* With transcendent wonder and holy fear, we can bow and worship in the reality of His Majesty. Through Jesus, we can draw near to God with a sincere heart in full assurance of faith; we can actually enter and abide in the holy place of God.